WHY DOES MY BODY DO THAT?

RUNNY NOSE

by Rachel Rose

Consultant: Beth Gambro
Reading Specialist, Yorkville, Illinois

Minneapolis, Minnesota

Teaching Tips

Before Reading
- Look at the cover of the book. Discuss the picture and the title.
- Ask readers to brainstorm a list of what they already know about runny noses. What can they expect to see in this book?
- Go on a picture walk, looking through the pictures to discuss vocabulary and make predictions about the text.

During Reading
- Read for purpose. Encourage readers to think about runny noses as they are reading.
- Ask readers to look for the details of the book. What are they learning about the body and having a runny nose?
- If readers encounter an unknown word, ask them to look at the sounds in the word. Then, ask them to look at the rest of the page. Are there any clues to help them understand?

After Reading
- Encourage readers to pick a buddy and reread the book together.
- Ask readers to name two things that can cause runny noses. Find the pages that tell about these things.
- Ask readers to write or draw something they learned about runny noses.

Credits: Cover and title page, © Pichai Pipatkuldilok/Dreamstime and © Download it/iStock; 3, © kdshutterman/iStock; 5, © RichLegg/iStock; 6–7, © dragana991/iStock; 9, © yodiyim/iStock; 10–11, © mrs/Getty Images; 13, © PeopleImages/iStock; 14–15, © Wavebreakmedia/iStock; 17, © Prostock-studio/Shutterstock; 18, © OoddySmile Studio/Shutterstock; 19, © Sharomka/Shutterstock; 21, © Imgorthand/iStock; 22, © Tetiana Lazunova/iStock; 23TL, © parinyabinsuk/iStock; 23TC, © Riska/iStock; 23TR, © nobeastsofierce/Shutterstock; 23BL, © Magic3D/Shutterstock; 23BC, © Suwan Wanawattanawong/Shutterstock; and 23BR, © yodiyim/iStock.

Library of Congress Cataloging-in-Publication Data

Names: Rose, Rachel, 1968- author.
Title: Runny nose / by Rachel Rose.
Description: Bearcub books. | Minneapolis, Minnesota : Bearport Publishing
  Company, [2023] | Series: Why does my body do that? | Includes
  bibliographical references and index.
Identifiers: LCCN 2022023090 (print) | LCCN 2022023091 (ebook) | ISBN
  9798885093378 (library binding) | ISBN 9798885094597 (paperback) | ISBN
  9798885095747 (ebook)
Subjects: LCSH: Runny nose--Juvenile literature. | Nose--Health
  aspects--Juvenile literature.
Classification: LCC RF341 .R67 2023 (print) | LCC RF341 (ebook) | DDC
  616.2/1--dc23/eng/20220516
LC record available at https://lccn.loc.gov/2022023090
LC ebook record available at https://lccn.loc.gov/2022023091

Copyright © 2023 Bearport Publishing Company. All rights reserved. No part of this publication may be reproduced in whole or in part, stored in any retrieval system, or transmitted in any form or by any means, electronic, mechanical, photocopying, recording, or otherwise, without written permission from the publisher.

For more information, write to Bearport Publishing, 5357 Penn Avenue South, Minneapolis, MN 55419.

Contents

A Cold Drip 4

See It Happen 22

Glossary 23

Index 24

Read More 24

Learn More Online 24

About the Author 24

A Cold Drip

I love playing in the snow.

But when I get cold, something happens.

My nose starts running.

Drip, drip!

Why does my body do that?

Everyone gets runny noses.

It is a healthy thing for your body to do.

How does it happen?

Your body makes sticky stuff called **mucus**.

It is in your **throat** and **lungs**.

Your nose has it, too.

Say mucus like MYOO-kuhs

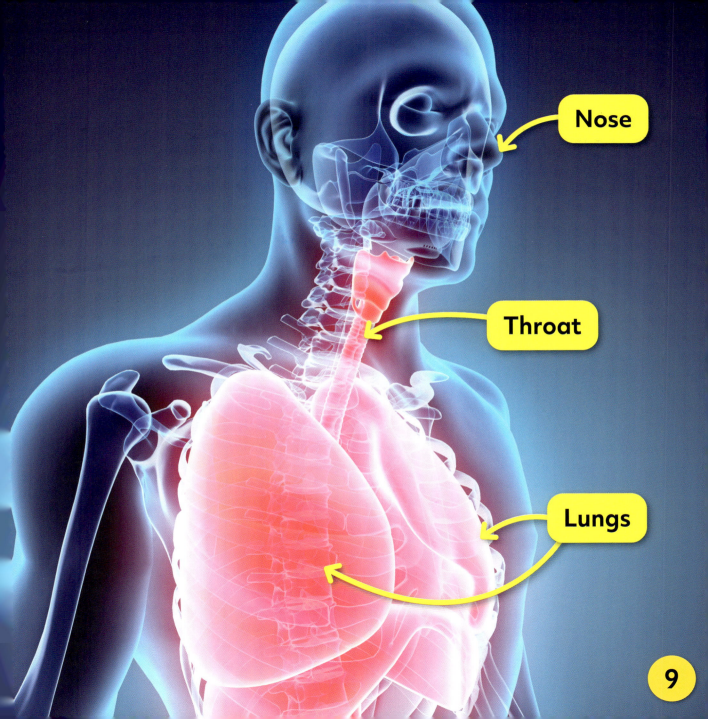

Mucus stops things from getting into your lungs.

Sometimes, your body makes too much.

It builds up as snot and runs out of your nose!

When does this happen?

It can be when you have a cold or the **flu**.

The mucus fights off **germs** that make you sick.

Runny noses happen in cold weather, too.

You breathe in cold air.

Then, your body makes extra mucus to warm the air.

Your nose may run when you are **allergic** to something.

This happens to some people near dogs or cats.

It can also happen near plants.

How can you stop all this runny snot?

The best way is to blow your nose.

Grab a tissue!

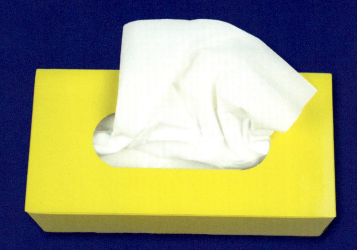

Sniffle!

A runny nose may bother you.

But it is a normal thing for your body to do.

It keeps you healthy.

See It Happen

There are tiny things in the air.

Your body makes mucus to stop them.

Extra mucus runs out of your nose.

22

Glossary

allergic having a body response to something

flu a kind of illness

germs tiny things that can make people sick

lungs parts of the body that help you breathe

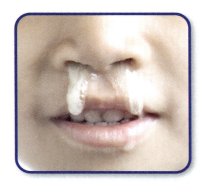

mucus sticky stuff from inside the nose and throat

throat the tube inside the neck

Index

allergic 16
germs 12
lungs 8–10
mucus 8, 10, 12, 14, 22
throat 8–9
tissue 18

Read More

Hansen, Grace. *Boogers and Snot (Beginning Science: Gross Body Functions).* Minneapolis: Abdo Kids, 2021.

Rose, Rachel. *Sneeze (Why Does My Body Do That?).* Minneapolis: Bearport Publishing, 2023.

Learn More Online

1. Go to **www.factsurfer.com** or scan the QR code below.
2. Enter "**Runny Nose**" into the search box.
3. Click on the cover of this book to see a list of websites.

About the Author

Rachel Rose lives in California. She loves to hike in the forest with her pup. Her dog doesn't make her nose run, but sometimes the trees do!